# Baby Owl
# Goes Away

Written by Jill Eggleton
Illustrated by Richard Hoit

Mother Owl
woke up.

"Come on,
Baby Owl,"
she said.
"We are going
to get dinner.
You stay with me."

Baby Owl
went away.

He saw
a hedgehog.
"I can get my
dinner," he said.

Baby Owl
saw a bat.

"I can get my
dinner," he said.

7

Baby Owl
saw a cat.

"I can get my
dinner," he said.

Baby Owl went up
to the cat.

The cat went after
Baby Owl.

"I will eat **you**,"
said the cat.

Mother Owl
came to help
Baby Owl.

She went after
the cat.

13

# Rules

# Guide Notes

Title: **Baby Owl Goes Away**

Stage: Early (2) – Yellow

Genre: Fiction

Approach: Guided Reading

Processes: Thinking Critically, Exploring Language, Processing Information

Written and Visual Focus: Rules, Speech Bubbles

Word Count: 127

## THINKING CRITICALLY

(sample questions)

- What do you think this story could be about?
- Focus on the title and discuss.
- Why do you think Mother Owl told Baby Owl to stay with her?
- Why do you think Baby Owl wanted to go off by himself?
- Why do you think it was dangerous for Baby Owl to be by himself?

## EXPLORING LANGUAGE

### Terminology

Title, cover, illustrations, author, illustrator

### Vocabulary

**Interest words:** owl, hedgehog, bat, rules, nice, woke

**High-frequency words (reinforced):** come, she, said, we, are, going, to, get, you, with, me, no, went, he, a, I, can, my, not, will, stay, away, saw, after

**New words:** eat, yes

**Compound word:** away

**Positional words:** up, on

### Print Conventions

Capital letter for sentence beginnings and names (**M**other, **B**aby **O**wl), full stops, quotation marks, commas, question marks, exclamation marks